COMPOSER
SHOWCASE
HAL LEONARD
TUDENT PIANO LIBRARY

Jazz Moods

EIGHT PIECES FOR PIANO SOLO

BY TONY CARAMIA

CONTENTS

ISBN 978-1-4234-3892-2

HAL•LEONARD®
CORPORATION

7777 W. BLUEMOUND RD. P.O. BOX 13819 MILWAUKEE, WI 53213

In Australia Contact:
Hal Leonard Australia Pty. Ltd.
4 Lentara Court
Cheltenham, Victoria, 3192 Australia
Email: ausadmin@halleonard.com.au

Visit Hal Leonard Online at
www.halleonard.com

Bluesy

By Tony Caramia

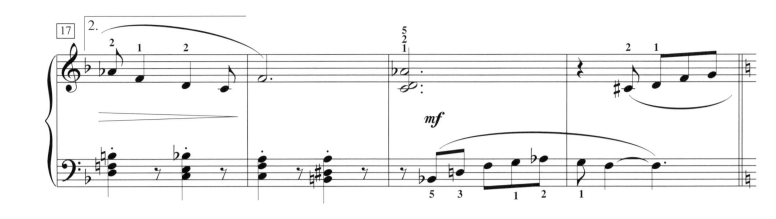

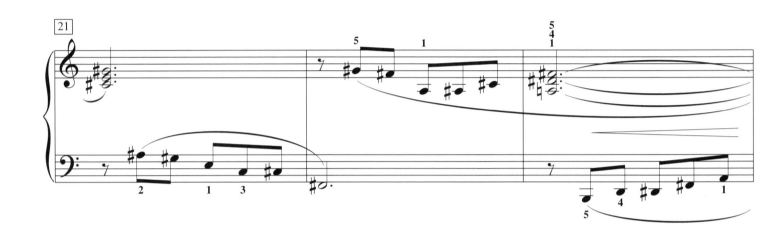

Carefree

By Tony Caramia

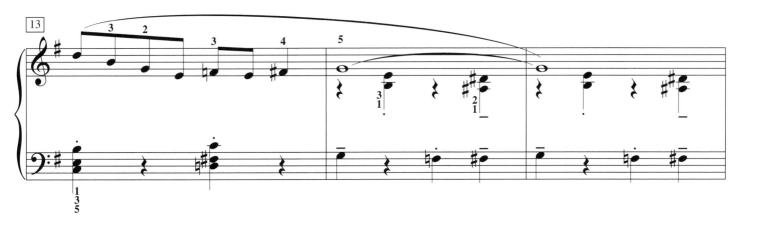

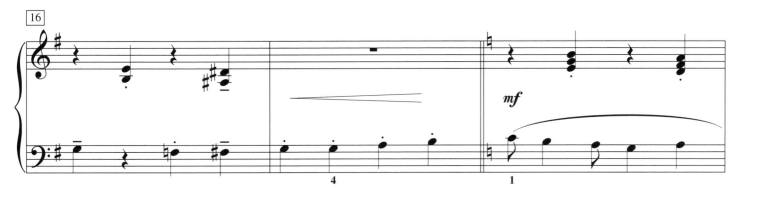

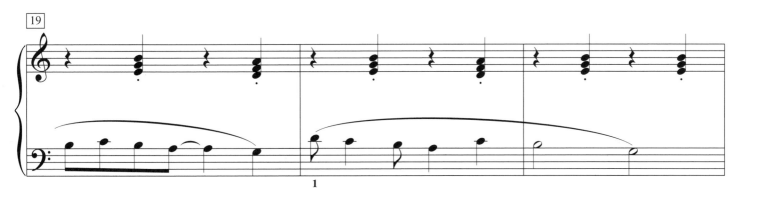

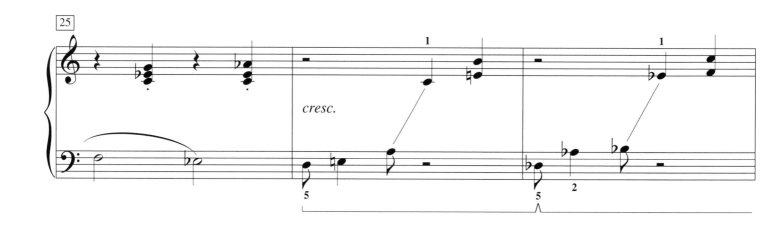

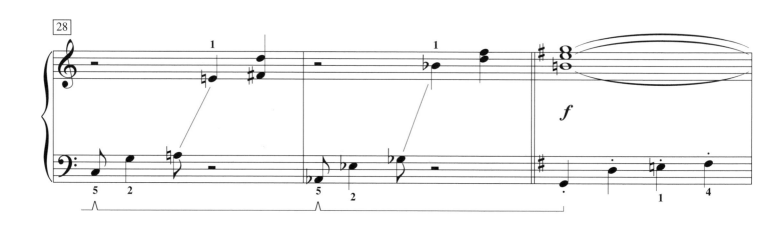

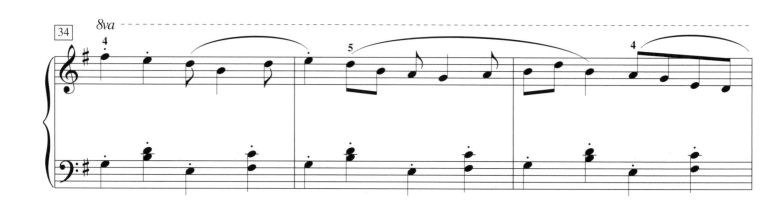

Groovin'

By Tony Caramia

With pedal

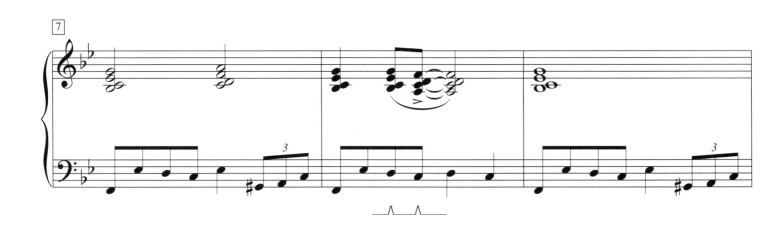

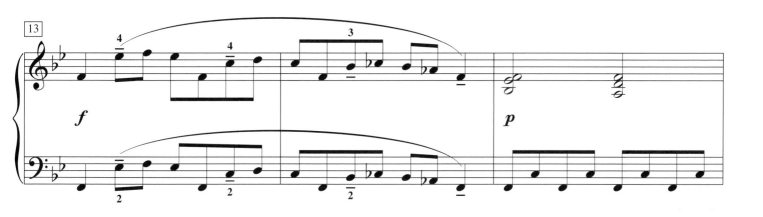

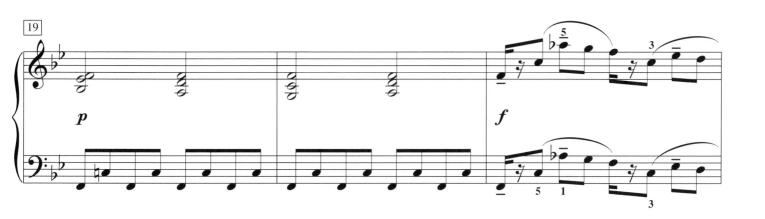

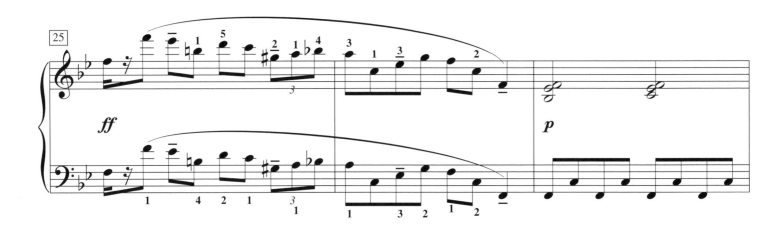

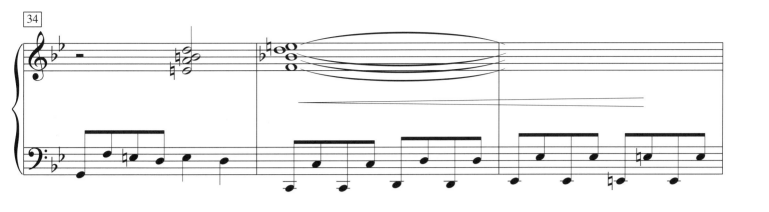

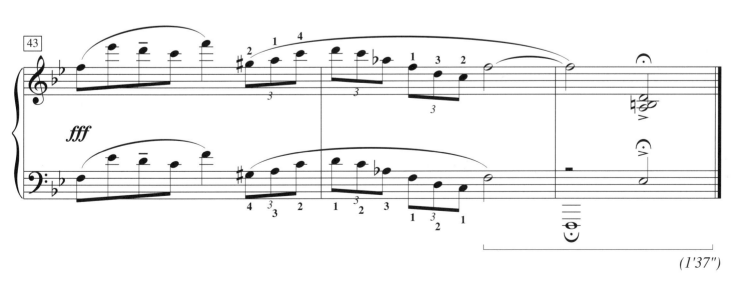

(1'37")

In a Singing Mood

By Tony Caramia

(1'09")

Snappy

By Tony Caramia

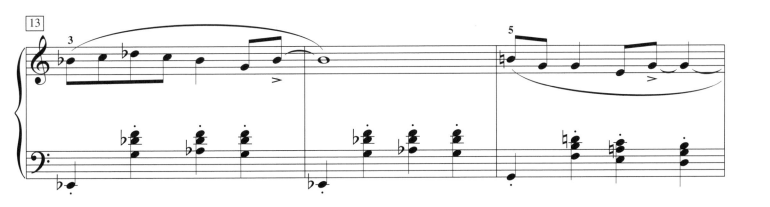

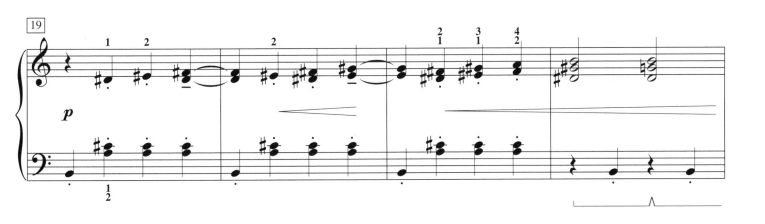

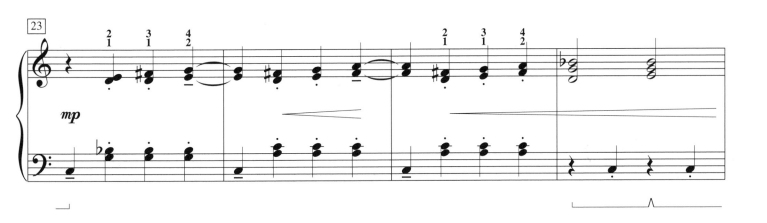

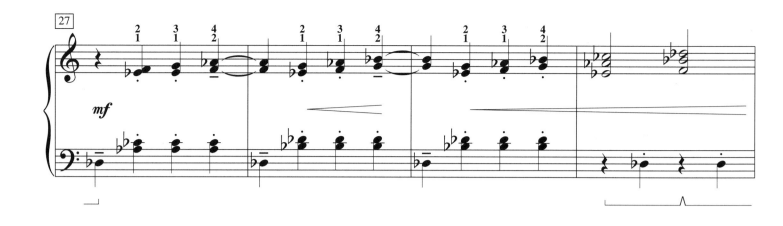

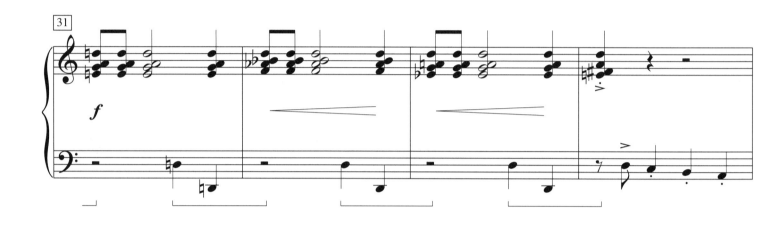

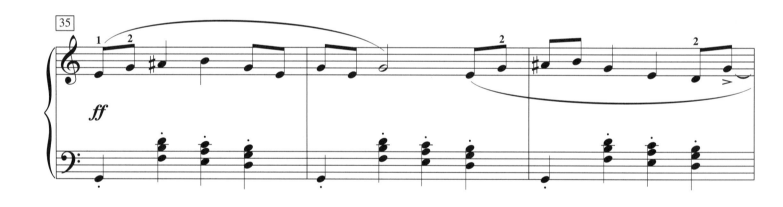

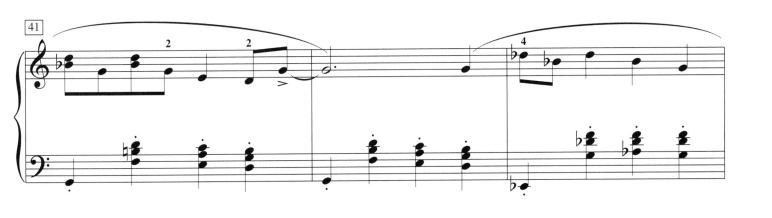

(2'07")

Spirited

By Tony Caramia

♩ = 72-80

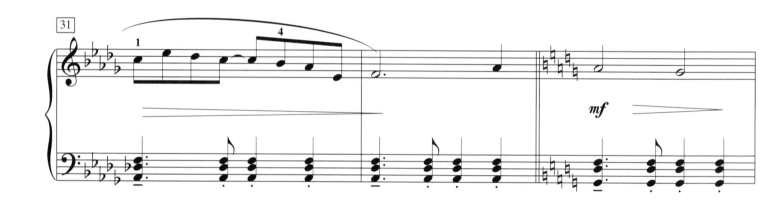

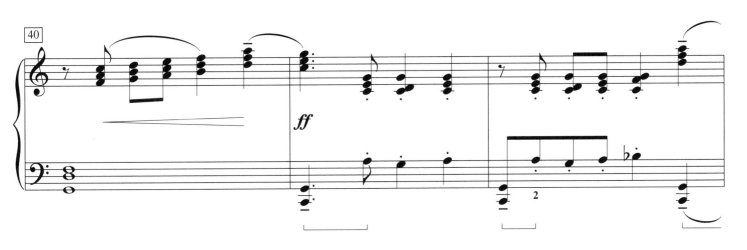

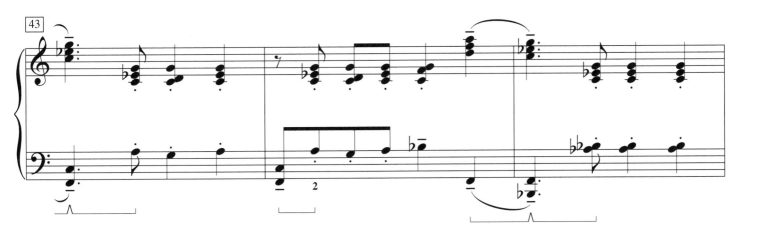

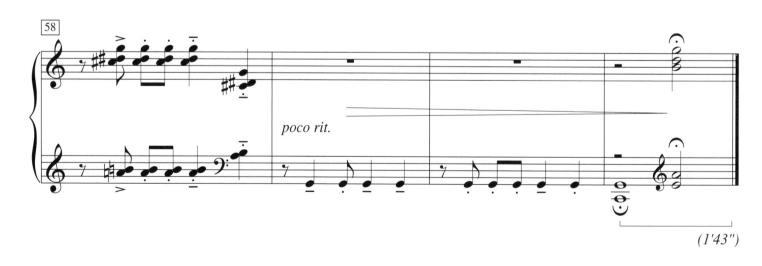

(1'43")

Whimsical

By Tony Caramia

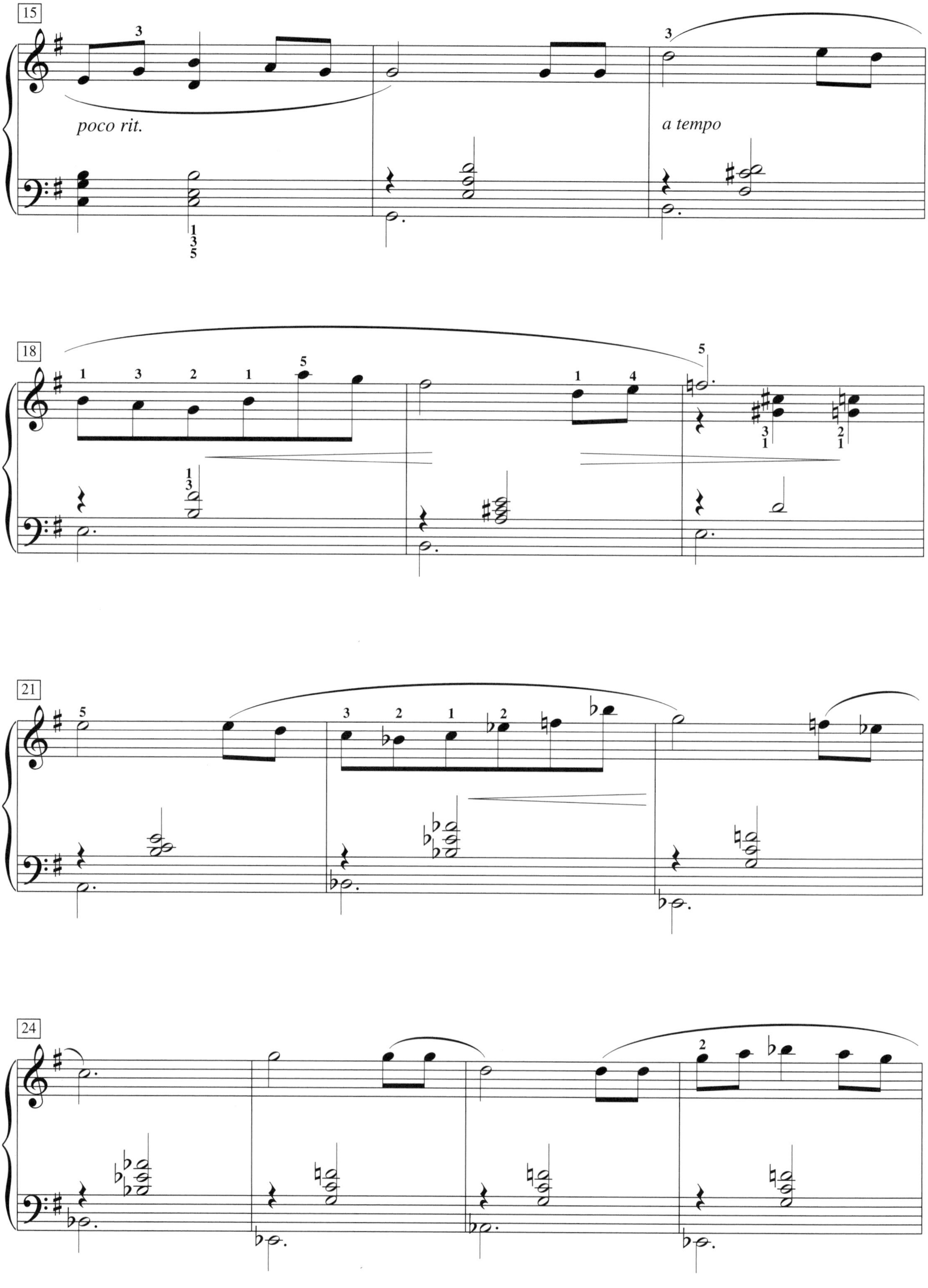
15
poco rit.
a tempo
18
21
24

broaden

ff   f   mf

mp   poco rit.

molto rit.   ppp

(1'34")

8vb ⌐

27

Walking Along

By Tony Caramia

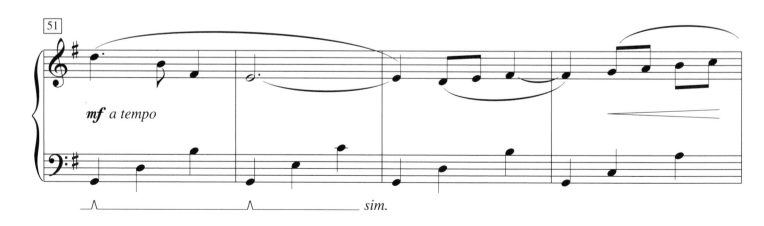

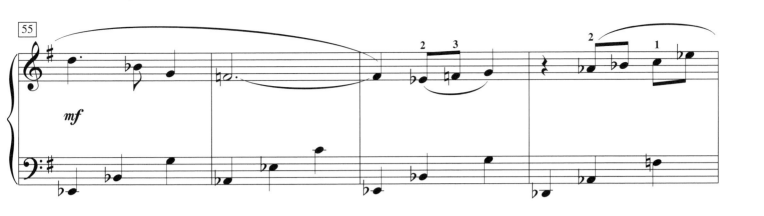

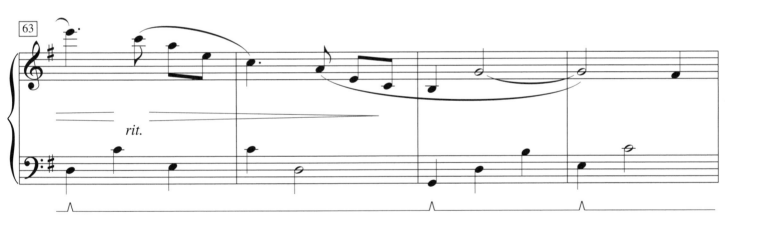

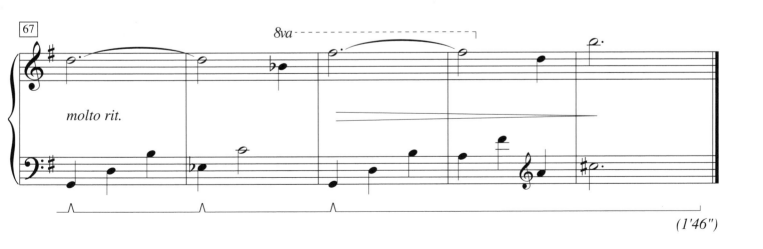

(1'46")

Notes from the Composer

Bluesy

This piece takes its title from several events:

- the use of minor thirds over a major chord (measure 1, beat 4; measure 3, beat 4)
- the use of minor thirds in a major sound (measure 5, beat 4)
- the minor third of a chord preceding its major third (measure 21, beats 5 and 6; measure 23, beats 2 and 3)
- the use of altered scale tones
    - lowered fifth: measure 6, last beat; measure 11, beat 4; measure 14, downbeat
    - lowered ninth: 1st/2nd endings, downbeat

The resulting clashes create a decidedly bluesy effect. In addition, the shuffling 6/8 meter suggests we're in no hurry. The constant harmonic shifts in the middle section (measures 19-34) give the left hand a chance to sing a blue melody. The Coda brings our bluesy journey to a dreamy, soft, and tender close.

Carefree

Here, the left hand plays a particularly important role, as it provides a steady pulse and sharply played sound, while exploring quickly changing harmonies. These left-hand rhythms and harmonies support a right-hand melody characterized by specific articulation markings. Try for an overall effect of sauntering down the street, smiling and offering friendly gestures to passersby. You should be in a good mood *before* you start this piece and your audience should definitely be all smiles when you finish!

Groovin'

Don't let the even-eighths notation interfere with the shuffle: this rhythm divides each beat into three. Emphasize the shorter notes and lean on beats 2 and 4 of each measure, especially when in unison. Strive for a big sound in the last nine measures.

In a Singing Mood

The title says it all: a soulful right-hand melody over a gentle accompaniment. Observe the dynamic markings carefully, as they point to special and important melody/harmony moments (the major seventh C♯ on the downbeat of measures 4 and 8; the minor seventh on the downbeat of measures 10 and 18). Be precise in the use of pedal; let the harmonic shifts be your ears' guide. Caress the keys in the last four measures: make the sound float away.

Snappy

While you strut along, ask a friend to snap his or her fingers on beats 2 and 4; lean on (don't accent) the sounds on these beats in both hands. This piece begins with staccato chords in the left hand: keep them light and steady. Swing the right-hand melody carefully: emphasize the shorter notes and observe the smooth phrases, creating nice contrasts with the snappy left hand. Measures 19–30 have many accidentals but the same pattern, creating a harmonic momentum that builds to measures 31–34. Then the real fun begins: notice the bluesy right-hand changes in measures 39–41, and the new key center starting at measure 43—all designed to add a buoyant and snappy finish to these happy sounds.

Spirited

Be sure to conserve your energy as you begin this piece, and pay close attention to the dynamic markings. "Spirited" grows through increased textures, higher dynamic levels, and wider distances between hands. At measure 25, lean on the downbeat left-hand chord while keeping beats 3 and 4 light, to add to the dance-like rhythms. If you'd like to make the accompaniment more interesting in this section, I suggest that in measures 26–27, 30–31, 32–33, 34–35, and 35–36 you connect the left-hand chord on beat 4 to the downbeat of the following measure. Be exuberant when you arrive at measure 41, but make sure you follow the dynamic changes in the measures that follow.

Walking Along

This piece is a gentle waltz that offers many contrasts to other pieces in this collection. Be certain to bring out the right-hand melody, while the left-hand interval on beat 2 is always tender. The smooth and flowing melody requires meticulous fingering. The pedal markings are designed to maximize the harmonic changes, so be sure to listen attentively to the results. In the final three measures, feel free to ad lib, using the G Lydian mode.

Whimsical

Another gentle waltz, this time with three-note chordal textures that add occasional dissonances. The phrases are long: do your best to go to the third measure of the phrase with a crescendo and then a slight diminuendo through the fourth measure. This piece was recorded on my CD, *Tribute* (www.cdbaby.com).